Praise for Sunil K. Gupta

Quick Results with the Output Delivery System is an excellent introductory text that illustrates the SAS Output Delivery System (ODS). Having little experience with ODS, I found this text extremely helpful for understanding how to get SAS to produce reports within the ODS framework. This text is a useful addition to SAS' excellent library of publications.

I liked Gupta's presentation style. He provides a nice balance of process flow and specific examples that give the reader a good introduction to ODS. I found this balance very helpful for understanding the aspects of the procedures. His writing is clear and precise. The combination of the writing, SAS code, and process flow diagrams will give a beginning SAS programmer a good background in ODS.

William Hewitt, Ph.D.
Senior Project Analyst, Fleet Credit Card Services, a subsidiary of FleetBoston Financial
Adjunct Professor, West Chester University

D1298215

SAS Press

Quick Results
with the Output Delivery System

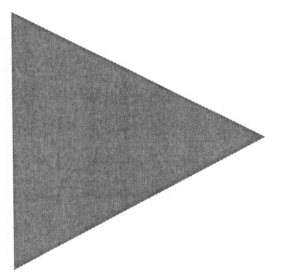

Sunil K. Gupta

The Power to Know.

The correct bibliographic citation for this manual is as follows: Gupta, Sunil K. 2003. *Quick Results with the Output Delivery System,* Cary, NC: SAS Institute Inc.

Quick Results with the Output Delivery System

Copyright © 2003, SAS Institute Inc., Cary, NC, USA

ISBN 1-59047-163-6

1st printing, February 2003
2nd printing, February 2005

SAS Publishing provides a complete selection of books and electronic products to help customers use SAS software to its fullest potential. For more information about our e-books, e-learning products, CDs, and hard-copy books, visit the SAS Publishing Web site at **support.sas.com/pubs** or call 1-800-727-3228.

Table of Contents

Acknowledgments

It is difficult to believe that I have come to the last page of completing my dream. Writing this book has been one of my greatest accomplishments that I will always be very proud of. I knew from the beginning that this major project would require the support and assistance of my family, friends, and associates.

I want to thank my wife, Bindiya, for always being there for me and cheering me on and my daughters Aarti and Anupama for being excited about the book. I want to thank John West, Judy Whatley, Stephenie Joyner, and Julie Platt of the Books By Users Program, and Art Carpenter, my editor for the Art Carpenter's SAS Software Series, for being great to work with and for making this book a valuable resource for SAS users. I want to thank my technical review team members at SAS, Sandy McNeill, Cynthia Zender, David Kelley, Bari Lawhorn, Jane Stroupe, Kim Sherrill, Chevell Parker, Dan O'Connor, Brian Schellenberger, Helen Wolfson,and Nancy Goodling, for their dedicated attention to all of the technical details. Finally, I would like to thank my peer technical review team members, Kirk Paul Lafler, Charlie Shipp, Curt Edmonds, Helen Wilfehrt, Sheree Anderson, Bob Hull, Deborah Testa, George Fernandez, Kim LeBouton, Patricia Gerend, and Dana Rafiee, for giving me ideas to improve this book.

Using this Book

Quick Results with the Output Delivery System introduces the concepts necessary for understanding and applying the new features of SAS' Output Delivery System (ODS). It discusses issues in defining and selecting destinations, selecting output objects, and enhancing reports with styles.

Chapter 1 provides an introduction to ODS. This chapter outlines the benefits of using ODS and reviews the basic structure of ODS statements. All of the ODS statements in this chapter are explained with examples in the other chapters.

Chapter 2 discusses the ODS destinations for report generation and how to write to them. Examples are provided for each of these destinations, including the HTML, RTF, PDF and PRINTER destinations. In addition, you can take advantage of destination specific options for greater control.

Chapter 3 discusses the details of how ODS creates and selects output objects. This is an important chapter for gaining an understanding of the basics of ODS. Examples are provided describing the use of ODS tools to identify objects and the options available to restrict results to a destination. In addition, a list of the object and object pathnames of selected SAS procedures is provided.

Chapter 4 discusses the OUTPUT destination and how to write to it. Examples are provided for creating SAS data sets. You can take control of the data set structure with additional options.

Chapter 5 discusses some of the power and flexibility of ODS that is inherent in the tools that are available for managing multiple objects created from SAS procedures. By knowing what options you have for referencing objects, you can be more selective in saving your results.

Chapter 6 discusses how to enhance reports with styles. With ODS styles, you can easily change a report's presentation attributes such as fonts, colors, and alignment. The selection of

SAS-supplied styles offers a variety of different styles that are appropriate for different destinations.

All SAS output files, listing outputs, and log files are generated with SAS Release 8.2 on the Windows 98 operating system. All examples are expected to work in batch mode and from the Program Editor of the SAS windowing environment.

Throughout this book, references are made to other sources of information. The heading "See Also" is used to point to other sections within this book that contain additional information on the topic. The heading "More Information" is used to indicate other SAS reference sources that contain information related to the current section.

CHAPTER 1

Introduction to the Output Delivery System (ODS)

1.1   What is ODS?

In SAS, a procedure or a DATA step supplies raw data and the name of a table definition that contains formatting instructions. Traditional SAS output is designed for a traditional line–printer. This type of output has limitations that prevent you from getting the most value from your results. ODS is designed to overcome the limitations of traditional SAS output. It provides a method of delivering output in a variety of formats, and makes the formatted output easy to access.

This book introduces the concepts necessary to understand and apply the basic features of ODS. It discusses the issues surrounding writing to destinations, manipulating objects, and enhancing reports with styles. The focus is on the creation of various types of output files through step-by-step examples.

1.2   Benefits of Using ODS

ODS opens a whole new world of choices in generating high-quality, detailed presentation output from SAS. With ODS, you can create various file types including HTML, Rich Text Format (RTF), PostScript (PS), Portable Document Format (PDF), and SAS data sets. You can also take advantage of ODS features to easily convert existing SAS code so that it can create these file types. In addition, the variety of styles available within ODS enables you to enhance presentation output by controlling the report's overall color scheme, font, and size.

The Results window of the SAS windowing environment in the following figure shows the various icons that represent the different files that can be created by ODS:

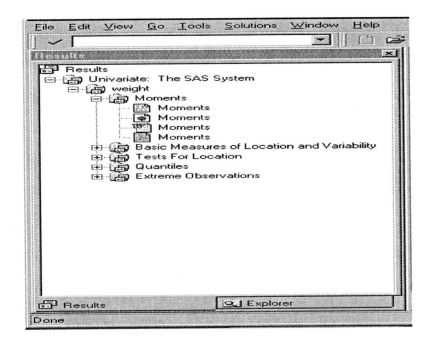

Figure 1.1   *Results window*

represents a Listing file.

represents an HTML file.

represents an RTF file.

represents a PDF file.

Through ODS, you can do the following:

- create HTML, RTF, PostScript, and PDF files

- select SAS-supplied styles to enhance reports

- create output objects from almost all SAS procedures

- create SAS data sets from output objects

- provide support for Web site navigation and management of HTML files.

1.2.1 Understanding ODS Terminology

When you are working in the ODS environment, it is helpful to consider the following ODS definitions:

- Destinations – Destinations are the locations to which ODS routes the output from SAS. ODS can be used to route quality presentation files, suitable for publishing, to various destinations, including LISTING (default), HTML, RTF, PRINTER, and PDF. ODS can also store results in a SAS data sets when you use the ODS OUTPUT statement. Destinations represent the output file type.

- Objects – Output objects are created by ODS to store the formatted results of most SAS procedures. An output object consists of the tabular data component from a SAS procedure and formatting instructions provided by a table template that is unique to that SAS procedure. You can select output objects to tailor your results.

- Styles – Styles define the presentation attributes of a report, such as font and color. ODS uses style definitions, or templates, to enhance the visual appearance of the output in those destinations that support styles. Note that styles do not apply to the LISTING and OUTPUT destinations.

1.3 Basic Structure of ODS Statements

The following is the syntax of some ODS statements that are essential for generating quick results with ODS. The numbers correspond to the explanations in the list that follows this syntax.

Example 1.1: Basic ODS syntax

ODS **TRACE** ON </<options>>;   ❶

ODS *destination* <FILE=*filename*>;   ❷

ODS **OUTPUT** *output-object-name=SAS-data-set-name*;   ❸

ODS <*destination*>**SELECT** *output-object-name*|ALL|NONE;   ❹

...SAS *procedure syntax*...   ❺

ODS <*destination*> **CLOSE**;   ❻

ODS **TRACE** OFF;   ❼

❶ The ODS TRACE ON statement is a useful tool for identifying output objects that are created from SAS procedures. You must place it before the first SAS procedure that you want to trace. Knowing what objects are created is important when you select objects for the destination.

❷ The ODS <*destination*> statements open a destination for output. A form of this statement is required to create the destination file. The *destination* value can be any of the destinations used for report generation, including LISTING, HTML, RTF, PS, and PDF. The FILE= option is required to name the output file for many of the destinations.

❸ The ODS OUTPUT statement creates SAS data sets. It saves the results that are stored in the output objects from SAS procedures to data sets. This is an alternative destination to the file types available in the ODS *<destination>* statements.   The object and data set names are required for this destination.

❹   The ODS *<destination>* SELECT statement specifies objects to include in the destination. This is an optional statement to restrict information to the destination.   An ODS SELECT statement can be created for each opened destination.   It is also possible to exclude objects from destinations with the ODS EXCLUDE statement.

❺   All results from one or more SAS procedures are routed to the open destination(s).   This is true for all destinations except the OUTPUT destination.

❻   The ODS *<destination>* CLOSE statement closes the destination.   You must close each opened destination to save results to that destination.   You can close all open destinations with the ODS_ALL_CLOSE statement.

❼   The ODS TRACE OFF statement turns off the trace feature.   Remember to place this statement after the last SAS procedure that you want to trace.

More Information

The *Complete Guide to the SAS Output Delivery System, Version 8* has detailed reference information about ODS syntax.

Chapter 2 of *Output Delivery System: The Basics* also has detailed information about ODS syntax.

You can also consult *SAS OnlineDoc* for more information about ODS syntax.

CHAPTER 2

Writing to Report Generation Destinations

2.1 Overview of Report Generation

ODS destinations for report generation include the following: HTML, RTF, LISTING, PRINTER, PS, PDF, and PCL. The HTML destination produces a quality presentation file suitable for viewing with a Web browser. The RTF, PRINTER, PS, PDF, and PCL destinations produce quality presentation files suitable for viewing and publishing. The LISTING destination produces the traditional SAS listing output.

The results of SAS procedures are routed to the ODS destinations as shown in the following process flow chart:

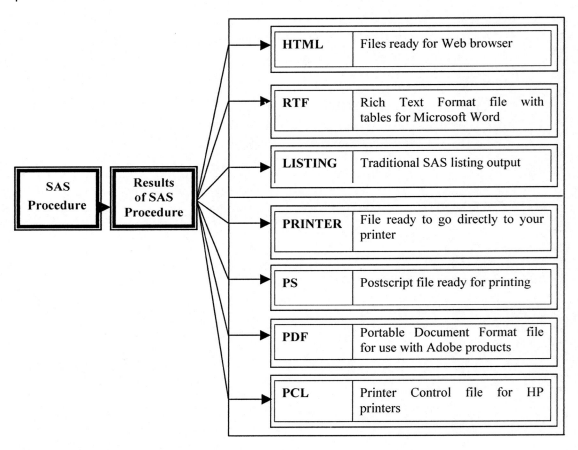

Figure 2.1 *ODS destinations for reports*

2.1.1 Creating HTML Files

ODS uses the HTML destination to create output that can be opened with a Web browser, such as Internet Explorer or Netscape Navigator. With ODS, you can easily create HTML files that support navigational functionality, content management, and Web site development without knowing how to program in HTML. Two key benefits of using HTML files are that they provide quick accessibility to current data and they provide the ability to access detail level information from a summary level graph by remote access. Since the HTML output is designed for viewing with a browser, it generally is not the best file type for high quality printing. In addition, there might be cases where an HTML file does not look good in Netscape Navigator because SAS Institute performs all tests using Internet Explorer.

Example 2.1: How to create HTML files

```
ODS LISTING CLOSE;  ❶

ODS HTML FILE = 'C:\ODSRSLTS\BODY.HTML';  ❷


PROC UNIVARIATE DATA=DEMOG;

    VAR WEIGHT;

RUN;  ❸


ODS HTML CLOSE;  ❹

ODS LISTING;  ❺
```

❶ The ODS LISTING CLOSE statement stops the routing of results to the default LISTING destination. You are not required to close the LISTING destination prior to writing to the HTML destination. In fact, you can write to more than one destination at the same time. The LISTING destination represents the traditional SAS listing output.

❷ The ODS HTML statement opens the HTML destination for output. This statement is required to create an HTML file. The FILE= option is used to name the destination HTML file. The BODY= option can be used in place of the FILE= option; they are interchangeable.

❸ The results of PROC UNIVARIATE are routed to the HTML file BODY.HTML. Note that PROC UNIVARIATE must be between the ODS HTML statement and the ODS HTML CLOSE statement to save the results in the HTML file. It is also highly recommended that you include a RUN statement at the end of each SAS procedure to establish step boundaries. In general, ODS statements act like global SAS statements and not like step boundaries between procedures.

❹ Once opened, a destination must be closed before the files that it generates can be used. The ODS HTML CLOSE statement is very important for ODS to write to the created HTML file and to make the HTML file available for viewing. Any result from SAS procedures that are called after the ODS CLOSE statement will not be saved to the HTML file.

❺ The ODS LISTING statement reestablishes the default settings and routes results to the LISTING destination. You must reopen the LISTING destination to view results from subsequent SAS procedures in the Output window.

The following is a portion of the HTML file that is generated by Example 2.1:

The SAS System

The UNIVARIATE Procedure
Variable: weight (Weight)

Moments			
N	25	Sum Weights	25
Mean	198.68	Sum Observations	4967
Std Deviation	44.5568177	Variance	1985.31
Skewness	-0.4326447	Kurtosis	-0.2970718
Uncorrected SS	1034491	Corrected SS	47647.44
Coeff Variation	22.4264232	Std Error Mean	8.91136353

Output 2.1   *Contents of BODY.HTML*

2.1.2 Creating HTML Files for Navigation

When creating HTML files, you can use advanced ODS features for navigational functionality. ODS enables you to create several interrelated HTML files (contents, page, and frame files) to better manage your results. ODS automatically integrates and creates the links in these files to specific sections of the body file, which stores your results. For example, the reader of the report can quickly find information by using the contents file because it creates a table of contents section that points to sections of the body file. This quick reference feature becomes beneficial when you have a large amount of information to organize and display. You can create any combination of these files as long as the body file is created. Creating the frame file requires the body file plus at least one other HTML file. The PAGE= option can be used to create an HTML file that references results by pages. It is generally not utilized as often.

Example 2.2: How to create body, contents, and frame files for better navigation

```
ODS HTML

    PATH = 'C:\ODSRSLTS\' (URL=NONE)    ❶

    BODY = 'BODY.HTML'    ❷

    CONTENTS = 'CONTENTS.HTML'    ❸

    FRAME = 'FRAME.HTML'    ❹

    NEWFILE = NONE;    ❺
PROC UNIVARIATE DATA=DEMOG;

    VAR WEIGHT;

RUN;

ODS HTML CLOSE;
```

The following figure displays the layout of the three HTML files that are created with the code presented in Example 2.2.

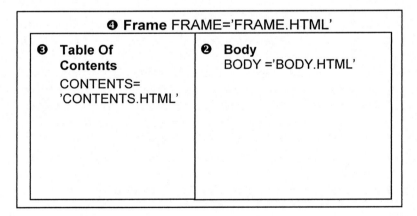

Figure 2.2 *Layout of HTML files*

The hyperlinks within the CONTENTS.HTML file reference sections of the BODY.HTML file. When a user clicks a hyperlink, the corresponding section is displayed in the Body window.

❶ The PATH= option specifies the directory folder that is used to store all the HTML files. The URL=NONE option enables ODS to create links with relative references instead of using physical file locations. With relative paths, a browser assumes that the frame, contents, and body files are in the same location on the Web server. It is recommended that you use the URL=NONE option with the PATH= option to facilitate the migration of HTML files to other locations, such as Web servers.

❷ The BODY= option is required to name the HTML file. The BODY= and the FILE= options are interchangeable.

❸ The CONTENTS= option creates an HTML file that forms a table of contents for the results. This HTML file contains hyperlinks, usually at the object level, that reference sections in the body file.

❹ The FRAME= option creates an HTML file that organizes the display of the body and contents files. Although any of the files can be viewed by the reader of the report, the frame file is usually opened for an integrated view of all files.

❺ You can combine the results of multiple procedures or steps into a single body file or have them written to a series of files. The NEWFILE= option defines when a new body file is opened for output. The names of the new body files are determined by using the BODY= filename as the common root name and then attaching a numeric suffix. The numeric suffix value is incremented by 1 for each new body file created.

Possible values for the NEWFILE= option include the following:

NONE   will not start a new body file (all the results go to a single file). This is the default setting.

OUTPUT   starts a new body file for each new output object.

PAGE   starts a new body file for each new page of output. This occurs when a procedure itself produces a page break.

PROC   starts a new body file for each procedure invocation.

BYGROUP   starts a new body file for each new BY group.

The following is a portion of the FRAME file that is generated in Example 2.2. Notice the table of contents on the left side with each object hyperlinked to the corresponding section within the body file. As a result, navigation of this information becomes much easier.

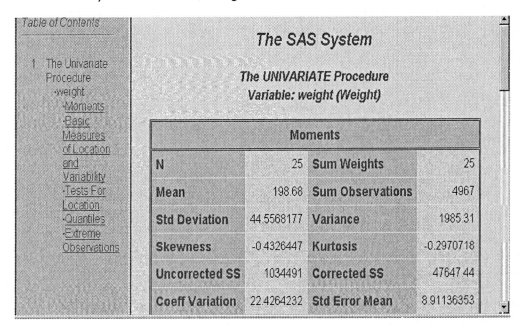

Output 2.2 *Contents of FRAME.HTML*

See Also
Section 2.2.1 "Routing Output from Several SAS Procedures to a Single Destination" shows an example of saving the results from PROC FREQ and PROC UNIVARIATE to the same HTML file.

2.1.3 Creating Graphs in HTML Files

When creating HTML files, you can use advanced ODS features to enable the user to access detail level information from a summary level graph. For example, a bar chart can be used to display summary level information that has hyperlinks to the detailed data that supports the graph.

Example 2.3: How to create graphs in HTML files

```
DATA DEMOG;

    SET DEMOG;

    LENGTH HTMLVARIABLE $ 40;


    HTMLVARIABLE = 'HREF=' || TRIM(DRUG) || '.HTML'; ❶
RUN;



ODS LISTING CLOSE;

ODS HTML

  PATH     ='C:\ODSRSLTS\' (URL=NONE)

  BODY     ='GRAPH_BODY.HTML'

 ;

GOPTIONS DEVICE=GIF HSIZE=5IN VSIZE=2.5IN; ❷



PATTERN1 V=EMPTY C=RED;

PATTERN2 V=X3 C=RED;
```

```
TITLE 'SUMMARY LEVEL: AVERAGE WEIGHT BY DRUG';

PROC GCHART DATA=DEMOG;

     VBAR DRUG / SUMVAR=WEIGHT TYPE=MEAN ❸

                              SUBGROUP=DRUG

                              HTML=HTMLVARIABLE;

     WHERE DRUG IN ('Active' 'Placebo');

RUN;

QUIT;

ODS HTML CLOSE;


ODS HTML

   PATH    ='C:\ODSRSLTS\' (URL=NONE)

   BODY    ='ACTIVE.HTML'  ; ❹


TITLE 'DETAIL LEVEL: LISTING OF ACTIVE PATIENTS';

FOOTNOTE '<A HREF="GRAPH_BODY.HTML">BACK</A>'; ❺


PROC PRINT DATA=DEMOG;

     VAR PATIENT DRUG WEIGHT GENDER RACE AGE HEIGHT;


     WHERE DRUG='Active';

RUN;
```

```
ODS HTML CLOSE;


ODS HTML

   PATH     ='C:\ODSRSLTS\'  (URL=NONE)

   BODY     ='PLACEBO.HTML'  ;   ❻


TITLE 'DETAIL LEVEL: LISTING OF PLACEBO PATIENTS';

FOOTNOTE '<A HREF="GRAPH_BODY.HTML">BACK</A>';


PROC PRINT DATA=DEMOG;

     VAR PATIENT DRUG WEIGHT GENDER RACE AGE HEIGHT;

     WHERE DRUG='Placebo';

RUN;

TITLE;

FOOTNOTE;


ODS HTML CLOSE;
```

❶ The variable HTMLVARIABLE is created to reference each of the detail level listings based on the value of the variable DRUG. The values of HTMLVARIABLE are the names of the detail-level HTML files (ACTIVE.HTML and PLACEBO.HTML). This information is used to hyperlink the summary level graph HTML file with the two detail-level HTML files.

❷ Setting the DEVICE= option in the GOPTIONS statement is required for ODS to use the appropriate device when it creates the graph. When you create the graph, the HSIZE= and VSIZE= options are useful for specifying the graph's dimensions in the HTML file.

❸ The summary level graph is created using PROC GCHART. The HTML= option is set to HTMLVARIABLE. This makes the bars in the graphs link to the HTML files they reference. If you want only the graph, then only steps ❷ and ❸ are required. The following is the HTML file that contains the summary level graph from Example 2.3:

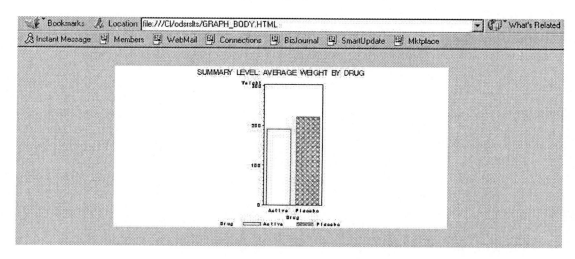

Output 2.3 *The summary level graph contained in GRAPH_BODY.HTML*

❹ The ACTIVE.HTML file is created. This file is the detail-level listing for the active patients. Since the summary graph has been coded to have hyperlinks to the detailed data used to make the chart, you can click the solid bar to display the list of all active patients as shown here:

DETAIL LEVEL: LISTING OF ACTIVE PATIENTS

Obs	patient	drug	weight	gender	race	age	height
1	001	Active	257	1	1	67.9	74.4
2	002	Active	168	1	0	36.7	63.1
5	005	Active	209	1	1	57.8	67.8
6	006	Active	116	0	1	47.5	56.7
7	007	Active	150	1	1	47.8	70.4
8	008	Active	172	1	1	82.6	68.5
9	009	Active	212	0	0	25.1	66.4

Output 2.4 *Contents of ACTIVE.HTML*

❺ In the footnote, a link is made back to GRAPH_BODY.HTML, the summary level graph HTML file. This allows you to return to the summary level graph. Every detail-level listing has this footnote.

⑥ The PLACEBO.HTML file is created.   This file is the detail-level listing for the placebo patients. You can also click the crosshatched bar in the summary graph to display the list of all placebo patients. In both of the detail-level listings, an additional hyperlink labeled **BACK** is provided in the footnote to return you to the original summary level graph.

Obs	patient	drug	weight	gender	race	age	height
3	003	Placebo	264	1	0	74.6	69.6
4	004	Placebo	270	1	1	73.8	63.2
10	010	Placebo	216	1	1	60.6	68.1
14	014	Placebo	179	0	0	37.4	74.7
19	019	Placebo	236	1	1	62.2	68.6
25	025	Placebo	162	1	0	56.1	72.4

BACK

Output 2.5 *Contents of PLACEBO.HTML*

2.1.4 Creating RTF Files

ODS uses the RTF destination to create Rich Text Format files to be read by Microsoft Word 2000 or later. Some of the key benefits of using RTF files include the ability to create tables, edit tables within the word processing package, take advantage of colors for more lively output, and control scalability and fonts within the word processing package. While the RTF file is not a Microsoft Word file, it can be saved as a Microsoft Word file from within Microsoft Word. In addition, other word processors might also read RTF files, but only Microsoft Word is supported by SAS.

Example 2.4: How to create an RTF File

```
OPTIONS ORIENTATION = LANDSCAPE NOCENTER NODATE;   ❶

ODS RTF FILE='C:\ODSRSLTS\DRUG.RTF';


TITLE  'Drug Freqs' ; ❷

FOOTNOTE1 'Active = Drug A, Placebo = Drug B'; ❸

FOOTNOTE2 'BioTech Inc., confidential 2001';


PROC FREQ DATA=DEMOG;

    TABLES DRUG;

RUN;

ODS RTF CLOSE;
```

❶ The ORIENTATION=LANDSCAPE and NOCENTER options in the OPTIONS statement are useful to define the page layout of the RTF file. The ORIENTATION= option offers great flexibility for wide tables and graphs. These options can be applied to the RTF, PRINTER, and PDF destinations, but must be specified before the destination is opened.

❷ The titles are placed in the header section of the RTF file. The following is the top portion of the RTF file generated by Example 2.4 in page layout mode.

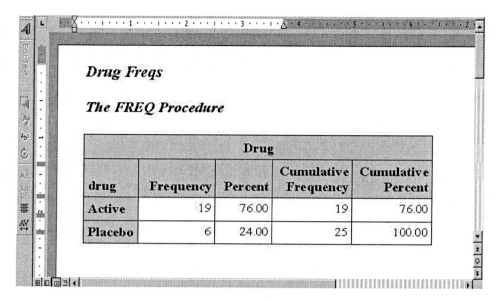

Output 2.6 *Header of DRUG.RTF*

❸ The footnotes are placed in the footer section of the RTF file. The following is the bottom portion of the same RTF file generated by Example 2.4 in page layout mode.

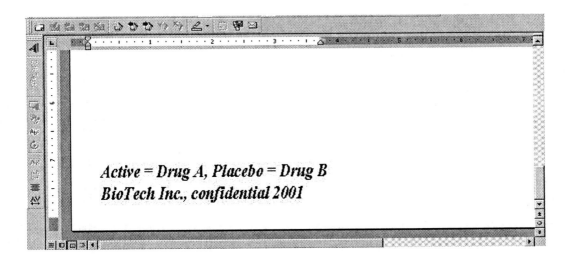

Output 2.7   *Footer of DRUG.RTF*

2.1.5 Formatting Text in RTF Files

When creating RTF files, you can use advanced ODS features to format the text. For example, you can use in-line escape characters or RTF control words to create superscripts, subscripts, and **Page** *X* **of** *Y* in titles and footnotes. By default, ODS places titles and footnotes in the header and footer sections of the RTF file, respectively.

Example 2.5: How to format text in RTF Files

```
OPTIONS ORIENTATION = LANDSCAPE NOCENTER NODATE NONUMBER;

ODS ESCAPECHAR = "^";    ❶

ODS RTF FILE='C:\ODSRSLTS\DRUG_FORMATTED.RTF' STARTPAGE=YES;  ❷


TITLE j=l "Drug Freqs^{super a}"

    j=r "{Page}  {\field{\*\fldinst{ PAGE }}}

        \~{of}\~{\field{\*\fldinst { NUMPAGES }}}" ;  ❸

FOOTNOTE1 '^{super a}Active = Drug A, Placebo = Drug B';

FOOTNOTE2 '^{sub BioTech Inc., confidential 2001}';


PROC FREQ DATA=DEMOG;

   TABLES DRUG;

RUN;

ODS RTF CLOSE;
```

❶ The ODS ESCAPECHAR statement defines the character to use for specifying in-line escape characters. The use of a unique escape character (such as ^) is recommended to prevent ODS from incorrectly formatting text. Once the escape character value is defined, it can be used to apply in-line formatting such as superscripts and subscripts in the HTML, RTF, PRINTER, and PDF destinations.

❷ The STARTPAGE= option in the ODS RTF statement controls when page breaks appear in the RTF file. The page break control feature provides you with the ability to decide which procedures will start on a new page and which procedures will stay on the same page. This option can be inserted throughout the program, as long as the RTF destination is open.

Values for the STARTPAGE= option include the following:

YES   starts a new page for each SAS procedure. This is the default setting

NO   prevents the starting of a new page for each SAS procedure.

❸ Once the escape character value is defined, you can take advantage of in-line formatting in titles and footnotes, for example.

The J= option in the TITLE statement justifies the alignment of the text. This option must be placed just before the text to be aligned. Possible values for the J= option include the following:

LEFT   aligns the text to the left side of the line.

RIGHT   aligns the text to the right side of the line.

CENTER   aligns the text to the center of the line.

`^{super a}` in the TITLE statement creates the superscripted letter a ([a]) at the end of the letters in **Freqs**. This [a] is referenced by the same [a] in the footnote.

`"{Page} {\field{\*\fldinst{ PAGE }}} \~{of}\~{\field{\*\fldinst { NUMPAGES }}}"` in the TITLE statement inserts **Page X of Y** in the title of the report.

`^{sub BioTech Inc., confidential 2001}` in the FOOTNOTE statement creates a subscript of the text **BioTech Inc., confidential 2001** in the footnote of the report.

The following is the top portion of the RTF file generated by Example 2.5 in page layout mode. Notice the left justified **Drug Freq** text with the [a] and the right justified **Page 1 of 1** in the title.

Drug Freqs[a]   *Page 1*   *of 1*

The FREQ Procedure

	Drug			
drug	Frequency	Percent	Cumulative Frequency	Cumulative Percent
Active	19	76.00	19	76.00
Placebo	6	24.00	25	100.00

Output 2.8 *Top portion of DRUG_FORMATTED.RTF*

The following is the bottom portion of the same RTF file generated by Example 2.5 in page layout mode. Notice the [a] with the text and the subscript of **BioTech Inc., confidential 2001** in the footnote.

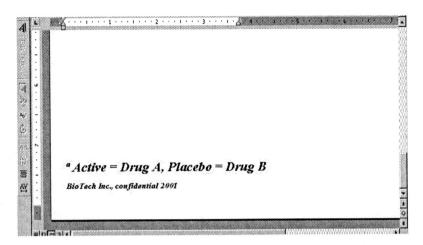

Output 2.9 *Bottom portion of DRUG_FORMATTED.RTF*

2.1.6 Creating Printer-Related Files (Printer, PS, PDF, and PCL)

ODS uses the printer-related destinations to spool files directly to a printer, or to send output to a PS, PDF, or PCL file. PDF files are readable by a viewer such as Adobe Acrobat Reader, and a PCL file is a postscript file format specifically for HP printers. The escape character text formatting feature introduced in Section 2.1.5 can also be used with the printer-related destinations.

The following example demonstrates how to create PDF files. The process for PS, PCL, and printer files, however, is very similar. Using PDF files offers an alternative to using HTML files for hyperlinking information. The advantages PDF files provide include better printing capability and better word processing features than HTML files. The ability to create PDF files also greatly simplifies the process of sharing documents between different operating systems. With one file format, you can publish via the World Wide Web, Lotus Notes, e-mail, and corporate networks.

Example 2.6: How to create PDF files

```
OPTIONS ORIENTATION = LANDSCAPE NOCENTER;


ODS PDF FILE='C:\ODSRSLTS\DRUG.PDF'; ❶


TITLE  'Drug Freqs';

FOOTNOTE1 'Active = Drug A, Placebo = Drug B';

FOOTNOTE2 'BioTech Inc., confidential 2001';


PROC FREQ DATA=DEMOG;

   TABLES DRUG;

RUN;


ODS PDF CLOSE; ❷
```

❶ The ODS PDF statement saves the results to a PDF file. By default, ODS automatically creates a table of contents based on the results of each SAS procedure using PDF bookmarks. To prevent the creation of the bookmarks, you can use the NOTOC option.

❷ Be aware that when first opening the PDF file after ODS creates it, you might see the message **Damaged file is being repaired**. This occurs because Acrobat Reader is reading an extra character in the file. The file is not really damaged. You can save the file from within Acrobat Writer software to prevent this message from displaying.

The following is the top portion of the PDF file generated by Example 2.6 in Acrobat Reader's page-only mode:

Drug Freqs

The FREQ Procedure

Drug				
drug	Frequency	Percent	Cumulative Frequency	Cumulative Percent
Active	19	76.00	19	76.00
Placebo	6	24.00	25	100.00

Output 2.10 *Top portion of DRUG.PDF*

The bottom portion of the same PDF file generated by Example 2.6 is shown in the following output in Acrobat Reader's page-only mode:

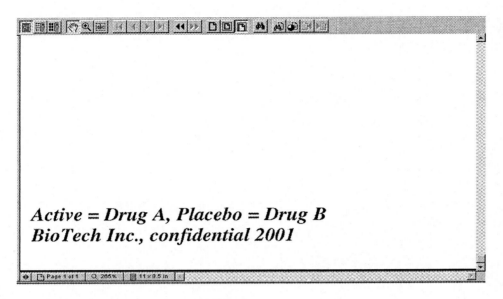

Output 2.11 *Bottom portion of DRUG.PDF*

2.1.7 Creating Several Printer-Related Files Simultaneously

When creating printer-related files, you can use advanced ODS features to create several files simultaneously. ODS can spool files directly to a printer and send output to PS, PDF, and PCL files in a single execution of a SAS procedure. This is accomplished with the ID= option. When each unique printer-related destination is opened with the ID= option, various ODS statements can be used for each destination individually. This is important because, in general, ODS can only write to one file for each opened destination. In-line formatting text can also be applied to create superscripts and subscripts, as in the following example.

Example 2.7: How to create printer, PS, PDF and PCL files simultaneously

```
OPTIONS ORIENTATION = LANDSCAPE NOCENTER;

ODS ESCAPECHAR = "^";


ODS PRINTER (ID=1);  ❶

ODS PS  FILE='C:\ODSRSLTS\DRUG.PS';  ❷

ODS PDF FILE='C:\ODSRSLTS\DRUG.PDF';  ❸

ODS PRINTER (ID=2) PRINTER='PCL5'

                FILE='C:\ODSRSLTS\DRUG.PCL' SAS;  ❹


TITLE  'Drug Freqs^{super a}';

FOOTNOTE1 '^{super a}Active = Drug A, Placebo = Drug B';

FOOTNOTE2 '^{sub BioTech Inc., confidential 2001}';


PROC FREQ DATA=DEMOG;

   TABLES DRUG;
RUN;


ODS PRINTER (ID=2) CLOSE;  ❺

ODS PDF CLOSE;

ODS PS CLOSE;

ODS PRINTER (ID=1) CLOSE;
```

The SAS log from Example 2.7 displays each printer-related file that is created or sent to the printer.

```
276    OPTIONS ORIENTATION = LANDSCAPE NOCENTER;

277    ODS ESCAPECHAR = "^";

278

279    ODS PRINTER (ID=1);

NOTE: Sending ODS PRINTER(1) output to printer "HP DeskJet 520
Printer".    ❶

280    ODS PS  FILE='C:\ODSRSLTS\DRUG.PS';

NOTE:    Writing    ODS    PS    output    to    DISK    destination
"C:\ODSRSLTS\DRUG.PS", printer "POSTSCRIPT".    ❷

281    ODS PDF FILE='C:\ODSRSLTS\DRUG.PDF';

NOTE:    Writing    ODS    PDF    output    to    DISK    destination
"C:\ODSRSLTS\DRUG.PDF", printer "PDF".    ❸

282    ODS PRINTER (ID=2) PRINTER='PCL5' FILE='C:\ODSRSLTS\DRUG.PCL'
SAS;

NOTE:    Writing    ODS    PRINTER(2)    output    to    DISK    destination
"C:\ODSRSLTS\DRUG.PCL", printer "PCL5".    ❹

283

284    TITLE  'Drug Freqs^{super a}';

285    FOOTNOTE1 '^{super a}Active = Drug A, Placebo = Drug B';

286    FOOTNOTE2 '^{sub BioTech Inc., confidential 2001}';

287

288    PROC FREQ DATA=DEMOG;

289        TABLES DRUG;

290    RUN;
```

```
NOTE:  PROCEDURE FREQ used:

       real time             0.44 seconds


NOTE:  There were 25 observations read from the data set WORK.DEMOG.


291

292   ODS PRINTER (ID=2) CLOSE;

NOTE:  ODS PRINTER(2) printed 1 page to C:\ODSRSLTS\DRUG.PCL.

293   ODS PDF CLOSE;

NOTE:  ODS PDF printed 1 page to C:\ODSRSLTS\DRUG.PDF.      ❺

294   ODS PS CLOSE;

NOTE:  ODS PS printed 1 page to C:\ODSRSLTS\DRUG.PS.

295   ODS PRINTER (ID=1) CLOSE;

NOTE:  ODS PRINTER(1) printed 1 page.
```

Output 2.12 *Partial SAS log for Example 2.7*

❶ The ODS PRINTER (ID=1) statement without a FILE= option sends the results directly to the default printer without saving the file. The ID= option assigns a uniquely named printer destination. When using the PRINTER destination without the FILE= option, make sure your printer is connected to avoid getting an error message.

❷ The ODS PS statement with the FILE= option saves the results to a postscript file. This statement is an alias for the ODS PRINTER PS statement.

❸ The ODS PDF statement saves the results to a PDF file. This statement is an alias for the ODS PRINTER PDF statement. The unique name of **PDF** is assigned to this destination. Note that when simultaneously creating multiple printer-related files, ODS does not create a table of contents in the PDF file.

❹ The ODS PRINTER (ID=2) statement with the PRINTER= option saves the results as a proprietary file type for HP printers (i.e., PCL). Since this destination is designated with ID=2, it can be distinguished from the ID=1, PS, and PDF destinations. Note that PRINTER='PCL5' specifies the HP printer and requires the additional SAS option at the end of the ODS statement.

❺ Remember to close each opened destination with the ODS PRINTER (*ID*) CLOSE statement or the corresponding alias statement. An alternative is to use the ODS _ALL_ CLOSE statement to close all opened destinations.

2.2 Routing Output from Multiple SAS Procedures

You will probably encounter a situation in which you need to route the output from more than one SAS procedure to more than one destination. You might be asked, for example, to save the results from multiple SAS procedures to an HTML file for viewing and an RTF file for editing. With ODS, this task is easy to accomplish. Instead of creating an HTML file for each analysis or rerunning the analysis to route the results to the RTF destination, ODS can easily save all of the results from SAS procedures to multiple destinations.

2.2.1 Routing Output from Multiple SAS Procedures to a Single Destination

All results from every SAS procedure that is run between the opening and closing of a given destination are saved to that destination. For example, you can include both graphs and tables in the same output file. The ODS statement to open the destination routes all output to the destination until the ODS statement to close the destination is executed. For the HTML destination, it is best to create several HTML files (body, contents, frame) for ease of navigation through all of the results.

Example 2.5: How to save output from several SAS procedures to HTML files

```
ODS HTML

        PATH = 'C:\ODSRSLTS\' (URL=NONE) ❶

        BODY = 'BODY2.HTML'

        CONTENTS = 'CONTENTS2.HTML'

        FRAME = 'FRAME2.HTML' ;


PROC FREQ DATA=DEMOG;

    TABLES DRUG;

RUN; ❷


PROC UNIVARIATE DATA=DEMOG;

    VAR WEIGHT;

RUN;

ODS HTML CLOSE; ❸
```

❶ The HTML destination is opened. For viewing the results of several SAS procedures, it is best to use the CONTENTS= and the FRAME= options for ease of navigation. After this statement, all results from procedures will be stored in the BODY2.HTML file and can be referenced by the FRAME2.HTML file.

❷ The results of PROC FREQ and PROC UNIVARIATE are saved to the HTML destination.

❸ Once the ODS HTML CLOSE statement is executed, the HTML file is completed and is ready for use.

The top portion of the frame file containing the PROC FREQ results is shown in the following output:

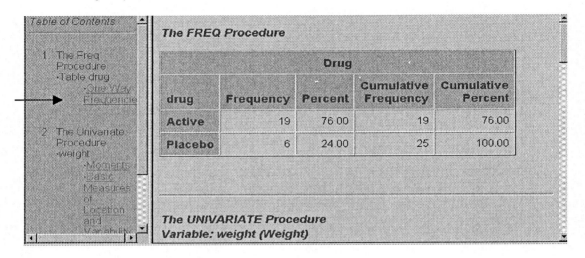

Output 2.13 *Top portion of FRAME2.HTML*

The bottom portion of the same frame file containing the PROC UNIVARIATE results is shown in the following output:

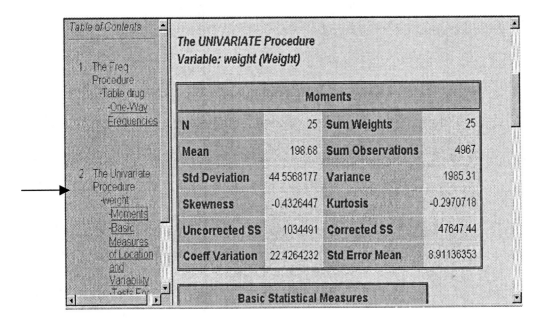

Output 2.14 *Bottom portion of FRAME2.HTML*

2.2.2 Routing Output to Several Different Destinations

Instead of rerunning an analysis to route results to an additional destination, ODS can save results to multiple destinations at the same time. You can accomplish this by opening multiple destinations with an ODS statement for each destination. Since destinations are independent of SAS procedure results, ODS simultaneously saves the results to each opened destination. In the following example, output is routed to HTML and RTF files.

Example 2.6: How to create an HTML file and an RTF file simultaneously

```
ODS HTML FILE = 'C:\ODSRSLTS\DEMOG.HTML' ; ❶

ODS RTF FILE= 'C:\ODSRSLTS\DEMOG.RTF' ; ❷


PROC UNIVARIATE DATA=DEMOG;

    VAR WEIGHT;

RUN;


ODS RTF CLOSE; ❸

ODS HTML CLOSE; ❹
```

❶ The HTML destination is opened for output. Results of PROC UNIVARIATE are routed to this destination.

❷ The RTF destination is opened for output. Results of PROC UNIVARIATE are routed to this destination.

❸ The RTF file is complete and ready for use.

❹ The HTML file is complete and ready for use.

Remember to have an ODS CLOSE statement for each destination that is opened. An alternative is to use the ODS _ALL_ CLOSE statement to close all opened destinations. This will also close the LISTING destination if it has not already been previously closed.

As you can see from the Results window of the SAS windowing environment, the HTML icon and the RTF icon correspond to the types of files created. Under each object icon , HTML and RTF destination icons are displayed because ODS opened both destinations for output. The information contained in each destination is the same. Note that the LISTING destination 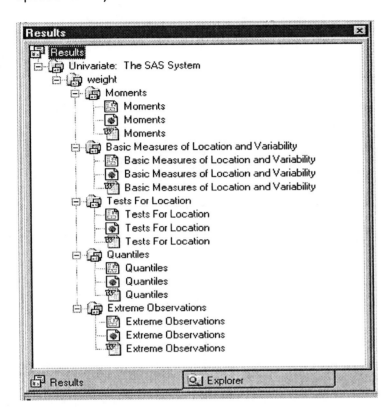 is also generated.   This is because, by default, the LISTING destination is opened unless you close it.

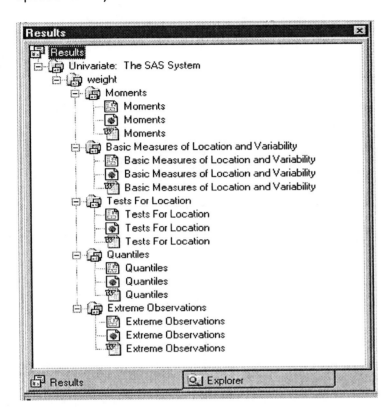

Figure 2.3   *Results window for Example 2.6*

More Information

Chapter 3 of *Output Delivery System: The Basics* has more information about creating HTML files for every SAS procedure, output, or page.   Information on drill-down features is also provided.   In addition, Chapter 5 of *Output Delivery System: The Basics* has more information about adding bookmarks to PDF files.

CHAPTER 3

Manipulating ODS Objects

3.1 Introduction to Output Objects

Output objects are the building blocks of ODS. These objects represent a new way to store the results of SAS procedures. ODS creates them from the execution of each SAS procedure. For example, PROC UNIVARIATE produces several output objects, including Moments and BasicMeasures, while PROC FREQ produces the OneWayFreqs object. Once these objects are created, ODS routes them to any open destination.

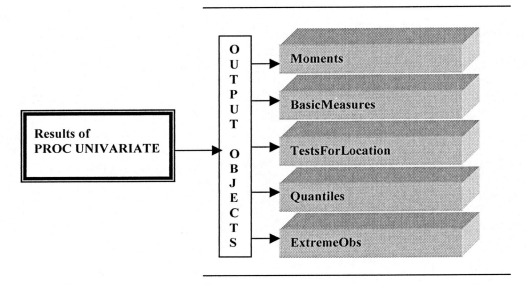

Figure 3.1 *Output objects from PROC UNIVARIATE*

Each output object consists of both data and table template components.

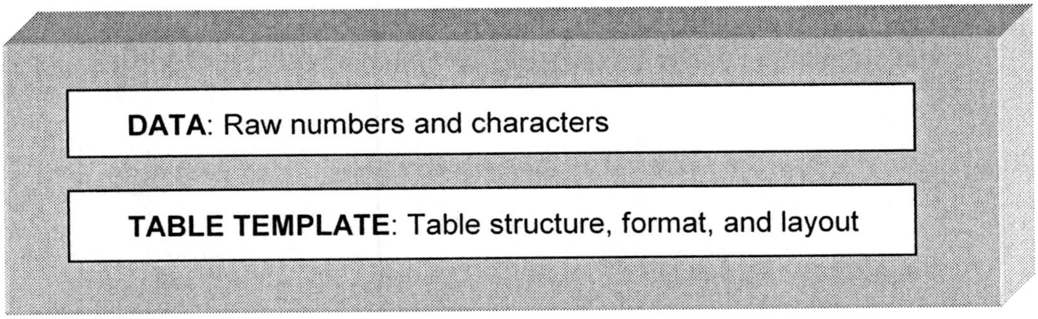

DATA: Raw numbers and characters

TABLE TEMPLATE: Table structure, format, and layout

Figure 3.2 *Output Object Structure*

The data component stores the raw numbers and characters of the output object.

The table template component stores the description of the format and the arrangement instructions for the output table structure. Almost all SAS procedures have a default table template for each output object created. The following SAS procedures are exceptions to this rule: PROC REPORT, PROC TABULATE, PROC PRINT, and PROC FREQ multiway tables. The table template defines the columns, layout, and format structure of the output table. Table templates do not, however, define the output's presentation information such as colors and fonts.

3.2 Identifying Output Objects with the ODS TRACE Statement

The ODS TRACE statement is a useful tool for identifying output objects that are created from SAS procedures. When working with ODS, you might first want to preprocess your SAS procedure with this statement so that you can identify all the objects that are created and then specify selected objects by name in other ODS statements. Using the ODS TRACE statement is important when you want to select specific objects for a destination.

Example 3.1: How to use the ODS TRACE statement

```
ODS TRACE ON / LABEL LISTING;    ❶


PROC UNIVARIATE DATA=DEMOG;

    VAR WEIGHT;

RUN;


ODS TRACE OFF;    ❷
```

The following SAS listing output from Example 3.1 displays information about the BasicMeasures object, which is one of the many objects created by PROC UNIVARIATE.

```
Output Added:

-------------

Name:       BasicMeasures    ❸

Label:      Basic Measures of Location and Variability    ❹

Template:   base.univariate.Measures    ❺

Path:       Univariate.weight.BasicMeasures    ❻

Label Path: 'The Univariate Procedure'.'weight'.'Basic Measures

of Location and Variability'    ❼

-------------
```

Output 3.1 *Partial ODS TRACE output*

❶ The ODS TRACE ON statement instructs ODS to start writing information to the SAS log for each output object created. The LABEL option is useful because it displays the object's label path attribute. The LISTING option is useful because it writes the information to the Output window instead of the SAS log. Writing to the LISTING destination might make it easier to associate the output object's name with the object's contents because the output object record is listed just before the results of each output object. Remember to place this statement before the SAS procedure to be traced.

❷ Remember to turn off the trace with the ODS TRACE OFF statement after the last SAS procedure you want to trace. This will stop the writing of trace records for each output object.

❸ The Name attribute defines the output object's name and is one of the most important attributes used to reference an object for selection or exclusion. The name attribute is generally indicative of the information it contains. There is another attribute called the Data attribute that only appears if it is different from the Name attribute. The Data attribute represents the data component that stores the raw numbers and characters.

❹ The Label attribute contains a description of the object.

❺ The Template attribute defines the name of the table template that is used to describe the table format and arrangement instructions. Once ODS creates the BasicMeasures object, it displays the contents of this object by using the instructions in the BASE.UNIVARIATE.MEASURES table template. You can use the table template name to customize the table structure.

❻ The Path attribute specifies the output object's path in the output hierarchy. It is the same information as the Label Path attribute, except that is uses names instead of labels. ODS uses a dot-delimited syntax notation to reference the object location within the SAS interactive environment and the batch environment. In general, the object's Path value is determined by the following naming convention: *Procedure-name.Group-name.Object-name*. *Procedure-name* is the SAS procedure name; *Group-name* is the group or variable name; and *Object-name* is the output object name. For example, based on this convention, the object's Path value, UNIVARIATE.WEIGHT.BASICMEASURES, means that the BasicMeasures object contains the PROC UNIVARIATE results of the variable WEIGHT.

❼ The Label Path attribute defines a long description of the object and is displayed with the LABEL option in the ODS TRACE statement.

The following table is an object reference table for selected Base SAS procedures. You can use it to identify objects without first preprocessing the SAS procedure to extract this information. The *X* in the Object Pathname column represents the variable's name used in the corresponding SAS procedure.

SAS PROCEDURE	OBJECT NAME	OBJECT PATHNAME
PROC FREQ	OneWayFreqs	Freq.*X*.OneWayFreqs
with LIST option	List	Freq.*X*_by_*Y*.List
PROC MEANS	Summary	Means.Summary
PROC SQL	SQL_Results	SQL.SQL_Results
PROC SUMMARY	Summary	Summary.Summary
PROC UNIVARIATE	Moments	Univariate.*X*.Moments
	BasicMeasures	Univariate.*X*.BasicMeasures
	TestsForLocation	Univariate.*X*.TestsForLocation
	Quantiles	Univariate.*X*.Quantiles
	ExtremeObs	Univariate.*X*.ExtremeObs
with NORMAL option	TestsForNormal	Univariate.*X*.TestsForNormal
with FREQ option	Frequency	Univariate.*X*.Frequency
with PLOT option	Plots	Univariate.*X*.Plots

Table 3.1 *Object reference table for selected Base SAS procedures*

3.3 Selecting Objects with the ODS SELECT Statement

After you have identified the objects, you can use the ODS SELECT statement to specify which objects you want to write to the destination.

The ODS SELECT statement instructs ODS to include only the specified objects in the selection list. The selection list acts like a filter that controls the output objects going to a destination. Each destination maintains a separate selection list. An overall selection list also exists and is applied if the destination-specific selection list is not defined. The object's name must meet the criteria of the appropriate selection list filters before ODS can process it.

With the exception of the OUTPUT destination, which utilizes a selection filter differently, the ODS SELECT statement is important because by default, all output objects are selected. This means that all results are displayed in all opened destinations.

Note: The behavior of the SELECT option with SAS procedures such as PROC COPY has not changed. That SELECT option is not related to the ODS SELECT statement.

3.3.1 The ODS Decision Tree Process

The steps below outline the selection process used by ODS:

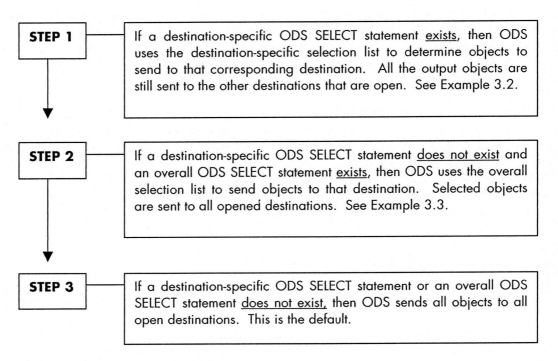

| STEP 1 | If a destination-specific ODS SELECT statement <u>exists</u>, then ODS uses the destination-specific selection list to determine objects to send to that corresponding destination. All the output objects are still sent to the other destinations that are open. See Example 3.2. |

| STEP 2 | If a destination-specific ODS SELECT statement <u>does not exist</u> and an overall ODS SELECT statement <u>exists</u>, then ODS uses the overall selection list to send objects to that destination. Selected objects are sent to all opened destinations. See Example 3.3. |

| STEP 3 | If a destination-specific ODS SELECT statement or an overall ODS SELECT statement <u>does not exist,</u> then ODS sends all objects to all open destinations. This is the default. |

Figure 3.3 *The ODS selection process*

3.3.2 Selecting Objects by Object Name

One of the easiest ways to select objects is by referencing the object's name. In the following example, all of the BasicMeasures results from PROC UNIVARIATE are saved to an HTML file. No other objects from this procedure are displayed in the HTML file. Note that any destination could have been used.

Example 3.2: How to select objects by object name for the HTML destination

```
OPTIONS NOCENTER;


ODS LISTING FILE='C:\ODSRSLTS\DEMOG.LST';

ODS HTML FILE = 'C:\ODSRSLTS\SELECT_DEMOG.HTML' ;


ODS HTML     ❶

         SELECT BASICMEASURES;   ❷

ODS HTML SHOW;    ❸


  PROC UNIVARIATE DATA=DEMOG;    ❹

      VAR WEIGHT;

  RUN;

ODS HTML CLOSE;

ODS LISTING CLOSE;
```

The SAS log from Example 3.2 displays the HTML selection list.

```
61    ods html select basicmeasures;  ❶  &  ❷

62    ods html show;

Current HTML select list is:

1. basicmeasures  ❸

63    proc univariate data=demog;   ❹

64     var weight;

65    run;



NOTE: PROCEDURE UNIVARIATE used:

      real time              0.05 seconds
```

Output 3.3 *Partial SAS log for Example 3.2*

❶ The HTML destination selection list is defined. If a destination-specific selection list is not specified, then the overall selection list is defined and applied to this destination. The selection list for the HTML destination is created when the HTML destination is opened.

❷ The ODS HTML SELECT statement lists the BasicMeasures object name to be included in the HTML file. All other objects created by PROC UNIVARIATE are excluded. Objects can also be selected by the object's pathname, such as UNIVARIATE.WEIGHT.BASICMEASURES. In this example, there is no difference in selecting the object by the object's name and the object's pathname. This is because all of the objects created in this example have a unique object name and a corresponding unique object pathname.

Choices for the ODS *<destination>* SELECT statement include the following:

ODS *<destination>* SELECT ALL
> Selects all objects for a specific destination.

ODS *<destination>* SELECT NONE
> Does not select any objects for a specific destination.

ODS <destination> SELECT *<OBJECT-NAME_1>* ...   <OBJECT-NAME_N>
> Selects specific object names. To select more than one object for a specific destination, list all object names separated by spaces. The object name can be any valid reference to the object such as the object pathname.

Remember to only select objects that will be created by the subsequent SAS procedure. Note that since the ODS SELECT statement is specified for the HTML destination, and the overall ODS SELECT statement does not exist, ODS will send all objects to the LISTING destination.

❸ The SHOW option writes information to the SAS log. All of the objects selected for the HTML destination are listed there. This is helpful to confirm the selection list.

❹ Although PROC UNIVARIATE creates all of its normal output objects, only the selected object, BasicMeasures, is written to the HTML destination. Since no selection list was defined for the LISTING destination, all output objects are still written to the LISTING destination.

The HTML file generated by Example 3.2 is shown in the following output. Notice that it contains only the BasicMeasures results.

The UNIVARIATE Procedure
Variable: weight (Weight)

Basic Statistical Measures			
Location		Variability	
Mean	198.6800	Std Deviation	44.55682
Median	199.0000	Variance	1985
Mode	.	Range	159.00000
		Interquartile Range	56.00000

Output 3.3 *Contents of SELECT_DEMOG.HTML from Example 3.2*

The listing output that is generated by Example 3.2 is shown in the following output. Notice that it contains all of the results.

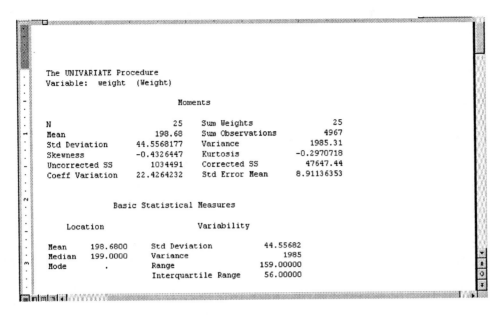

```
The UNIVARIATE Procedure
Variable:  weight  (Weight)

                          Moments

N                       25   Sum Weights              25
Mean                198.68   Sum Observations       4967
Std Deviation   44.5568177   Variance            1985.31
Skewness        -0.4326447   Kurtosis         -0.2970718
Uncorrected SS     1034491   Corrected SS       47647.44
Coeff Variation 22.4264232   Std Error Mean    8.91136353


              Basic Statistical Measures

     Location                    Variability

Mean     198.6800   Std Deviation          44.55682
Median   199.0000   Variance                   1985
Mode        .       Range               159.00000
                    Interquartile Range  56.00000
```

Output 3.4 *Contents of DEMOG.LST*

Example 3.3: How to select objects by object name for all destinations

```
OPTIONS NOCENTER;


ODS LISTING FILE='C:\ODSRSLTS\SELECT_DEMOG.LST';

ODS HTML FILE = 'C:\ODSRSLTS\SELECT_DEMOG.HTML' ;


ODS     ❶

        SELECT BASICMEASURES;   ❷

ODS SHOW;   ❸


 PROC UNIVARIATE DATA=DEMOG;   ❹
```

```
      VAR WEIGHT;

 RUN;

ODS HTML CLOSE;

ODS LISTING CLOSE;
```

The SAS log from Example 3.3 displays the HTML selection list.

```
61    ods select basicmeasures; ❶ & ❷

62    ods show;

Current OVERALL select list is:

1. basicmeasures ❸

63    proc univariate data=demog; ❹

64    var weight;

65    run;



NOTE: PROCEDURE UNIVARIATE used:

      real time            0.05 seconds
```

Output 3.5 *Partial SAS log for Example 3.3*

❶ The overall selection list is defined. Since a destination specific selection list is not specified, the overall selection list is applied to all opened destinations. In this example, both the HTML and listing files contain only the selected objects.

❷ The ODS SELECT statement lists the BasicMeasures object name to be included in all output files. All other objects created by PROC UNIVARIATE are excluded from all output files.

Choices for the overall ODS SELECT statement include the following:

ODS SELECT ALL
> Selects all objects for all destinations.

ODS SELECT NONE
> Does not select any objects for any destination.

ODS SELECT *<OBJECT-NAME-1>* ...   *<OBJECT-NAME-N>;*
> Selects specific object names.   To select more than one object for all destinations, list all object names separated by spaces.   The object name can be any valid reference to the object such as the object pathname.

❸ The SHOW option writes information to the SAS log. All of the objects selected for the output files are listed there. This is helpful to confirm the overall selection list.

❹ Although PROC UNIVARIATE creates all of its normal output objects, only the selected object, BasicMeasures, is written to the HTML and LISTING destinations.

The HTML file generated by Example 3.3 is shown in the following output:

The UNIVARIATE Procedure
Variable: weight (Weight)

Basic Statistical Measures			
Location		Variability	
Mean	198.6800	Std Deviation	44.55682
Median	199.0000	Variance	1985
Mode		Range	159.00000
		Interquartile Range	56.00000

Output 3.6 *Contents of SELECT_DEMOG.HTML for Example 3.3*

The listing output generated by Example 3.3 is shown in the following output. Notice that both the HTML and listing output contain only the BasicMeasures results.

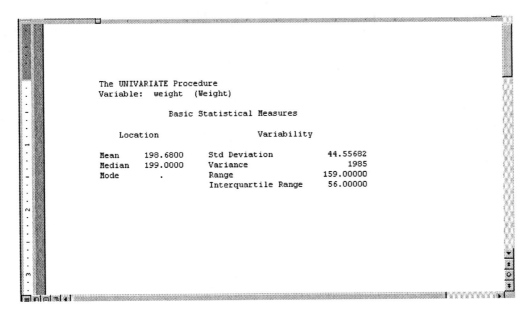

```
The UNIVARIATE Procedure
Variable:  weight  (Weight)

              Basic Statistical Measures

      Location                    Variability

Mean     198.6800   Std Deviation          44.55682
Median   199.0000   Variance                   1985
Mode          .     Range              159.00000
                    Interquartile Range  56.00000
```

Output 3.7 *Contents of SELECT_DEMOG.LST*

3.4 Excluding Objects with the ODS EXCLUDE Statement

An alternative to selecting objects is to exclude objects. Sometimes it might be easier to specify objects to exclude instead of listing all of the objects to include in the selection list. Excluding objects from the output file is accomplished with the ODS EXCLUDE statement. In the following example, all objects except the BasicMeasures object are included in an HTML file.

Example 3.4: How to exclude objects

```
ODS HTML FILE = 'C:\ODSRSLTS\EXCLUDE_DEMOG.HTML';

ODS HTML EXCLUDE BASICMEASURES;  ❶

ODS HTML SHOW;


PROC UNIVARIATE DATA=DEMOG;

    VAR WEIGHT;

RUN;

ODS HTML CLOSE;
```

The SAS log from Example 3.4 displays the HTML exclusion list.

```
117   ods html exclude basicmeasures;

118   ods html show;

Current HTML exclude list is:

1. basicmeasures  ❶

119   proc univariate data=demog;

120    var weight;

run;
```

Output 3.8 *Partial SAS log for Example 3.4*

❶ The ODS HTML EXCLUDE statement excludes the BasicMeasures object from the HTML file. All other objects created by PROC UNIVARIATE are included.

The choices that were displayed for the ODS SELECT statement in Example 3.2 are also available with the ODS EXCLUDE statement.

3.5 Maintaining a Constant Selection List with the PERSIST Option

The default behavior of ODS is to reset the selection or exclusion list after the step boundary of each SAS procedure. You might, however, have the need to keep the selection and exclusion lists for several procedure invocations. To override the default behavior, use the PERSIST option to maintain the selection list after a step boundary, such as a RUN or a QUIT statement.

Example 3.5: How to use the PERSIST option to maintain a selection list

```
ODS HTML  FILE = 'C:\ODSRSLTS\SELECT_PERSIST_DEMOG.HTML' ;

ODS HTML SELECT BASICMEASURES(PERSIST) EXTREMEOBS;    ❶

ODS HTML SHOW;


TITLE 'RUN 1 - BasicMeasures and Extremeobs objects are selected';

PROC UNIVARIATE DATA=DEMOG;

     VAR WEIGHT;

RUN;   ❷

ODS HTML SHOW;


TITLE 'RUN 2 - BasicMeasures object is still selected';

PROC UNIVARIATE DATA=DEMOG;   ❸

     VAR WEIGHT;

RUN;

ODS HTML CLOSE;
```

The SAS log from Example 3.5 displays the HTML selection list after each execution of PROC UNIVARIATE.

```
125   ods html select basicmeasures (persist) extremeobs;   ❶

126   ods html show;

Current HTML select list is:

1. basicmeasures(PERSIST)

2. extremeobs

127    title 'Run 1 -  BasicMeasures  and  Extremeobs  objects  are
selected';

128   proc univariate data=demog;

129    var weight;

130   run;


NOTE:  PROCEDURE UNIVARIATE used:

       real time              0.10 seconds


131   ods html show;

Current HTML select list is:

1. basicmeasures(PERSIST)  ❷

132    title 'Run 2 - BasicMeasures object is still selected';

133   proc univariate data=demog;  ❸

134    var weight;

135   run;

NOTE:  PROCEDURE UNIVARIATE used:

       real time              0.04 seconds
```

Output 3.9 *Partial SAS log for Example 3.5*

❶ The PERSIST option follows the object name, BasicMeasures. This informs ODS to maintain the BasicMeasures object in the selection list across step boundaries, but not the ExtremeObs object. You can apply the PERSIST option to any object.

❷ The RUN statement is the first step boundary after the ODS HTML SELECT statement. At this point, the HTML selection list would normally be reset to include all objects. However, with the PERSIST option indicated, the BasicMeasures object is the only object selected. Note that although the ExtremeObs object was in the ODS SELECT statement before the execution of the first PROC UNIVARIATE, it is no longer selected when the second PROC UNIVARIATE is executed. It is not selected because the PERSIST option was not used for the ExtremeObs output object.

❸ In the second execution of PROC UNIVARIATE, only the BasicMeasures object is included in the HTML file. When you are using the PERSIST option and you change the SAS procedure, you need to reset the selection list to ALL to be able to clear the selection list so that all output objects will again be sent to the HTML destination. This is accomplished with the ODS HTML SELECT ALL statement.

Note that it is possible to obtain unpredictable results when mixing ODS SELECT and ODS EXCLUDE statements, especially if you have also specified the PERSIST option.

See Also

Section 5.2 "Managing Multiple Objects Generated with BY Statements" shows examples of selecting objects by pathname.

CHAPTER 4

Writing to the OUTPUT Destination

4.1 Overview of the OUTPUT Destination

The ODS destination for creating data sets is the OUTPUT destination. This destination enables you to store your procedure results for further analysis. Unlike ODS destinations for report generation, with the OUTPUT destination you must select at least one output object because the default is to exclude all output objects.

The results of SAS procedures are routed to the OUTPUT destination as shown in the following process flow chart:

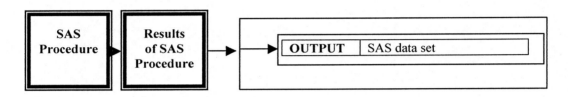

Figure 4.1 *Routing of the OUTPUT destination*

4.2 Creating Data Sets

ODS enables you to save almost any part of any SAS procedure output as a SAS data set. For example, programmers can create SAS data sets to save the statistics generated from statistical procedures. One of the advantages of using ODS to create SAS data sets instead of using the OUT= option with regular SAS code is that ODS provides additional options for saving objects to multiple SAS data sets. In addition, not all SAS procedures support the OUT= option, while any SAS procedure that uses table templates for output objects can produce an output data set.

Example 4.1: How to create SAS data sets with ODS

```
ODS OUTPUT BASICMEASURES = MYLIB.MEASURE;  ❶
```

```
PROC UNIVARIATE DATA=DEMOG;

    VAR WEIGHT;

RUN;
```

```
ODS OUTPUT CLOSE;  ❷
```

The SAS listing output from Example 4.1 displays the contents and observations of the data set that is created.

```
* Proc contents of MYLIB.MEASURE Output Data Set;


#     Variable        Type    Len    Pos    Format
_____

2     LocMeasure      Char      6     22

3     LocValue        Num       8      0    8.4

4     VarMeasure      Char     19     28

1     VarName         Char      6     16

5     VarValue        Num       8      8    D10.


* Proc print of MYLIB.MEASURE Output Data Set;


            Measure as SAS Data set


       Var       Loc
Obs    Name    Measure LocValue  VarMeasure    VarValue


 1    weight   Mean    198.6800  Std Deviation       44.55682

 2    weight   Median  199.0000  Variance                1985

 3    weight   Mode        .     Range           159.00000

 4    weight            _        Interquartile Range 56.00000
```

Output 4.1 *Partial listing output from Example 4.1*

❶ The ODS OUTPUT statement creates the SAS data set MYLIB.MEASURE. Since the OUTPUT destination requires that you specify an object's name, it is useful to use Table 3.1 "Object Reference table for selected Base SAS procedures" or the ODS TRACE output to obtain this information. In this example, the BasicMeasures object is selected to be included in the data set. That is, the MYLIB.MEASURE data set contains the BasicMeasures results from PROC UNIVARIATE.

You can repeat the *object-name = data-set-name* syntax in the same ODS OUTPUT statement to save other objects as data sets. Each object and data set name pair must be separated from others by spaces. Remember to place the ODS OUTPUT statement immediately before the associated SAS procedure. The usual data set options, such as RENAME=, DROP=, and WHERE=, can also be used in the ODS OUTPUT statement.

❷ The ODS OUTPUT CLOSE statement closes the OUTPUT destination and makes the data set available for access. Only one ODS OUTPUT CLOSE statement is needed even if you create multiple data sets. Also, at a step boundary ODS automatically resets the OUTPUT destination to EXCLUDE ALL. Although the ODS OUTPUT CLOSE statement is therefore not necessary, it can be explicitly included for code completeness.

4.3 Creating Multiple Data Sets

You can use advanced ODS features to create multiple data sets. For example, you can create a data set that stores all of the information of an analysis, or create separate data sets for each object selected using the MATCH_ALL option. The default is that all data for an object goes into one data set. In addition, a macro variable can be created to store the names of each data set created. This makes it easy to append the data sets using the DATA step, if needed.

Example 4.2: How to create multiple SAS data sets with ODS

```
ODS OUTPUT BASICMEASURES(MATCH_ALL = MEASURE_DSN) = MYLIB.MEASURE;  ❶

PROC UNIVARIATE DATA=DEMOG;

     VAR WEIGHT HEIGHT;  ❷

RUN;



ODS OUTPUT CLOSE;



%PUT The MEASURE_DSN macro variable contains the following data sets
&MEASURE_DSN..;
```

The SAS log from Example 4.2 displays the two data sets that are created.

```
11          ODS     OUTPUT     BASICMEASURES(MATCH_ALL=      MEASURE_DSN)      =
MYLIB.MEASURE;

12

13    PROC UNIVARIATE DATA=DEMOG;

14     VAR WEIGHT HEIGHT;

15    RUN;



NOTE:  The  data  set  MYLIB.MEASURE  has  4  observations  and  5
variables.  ❷

NOTE:  The  data  set  MYLIB.MEASURE1  has  4  observations  and  5
variables.

NOTE: PROCEDURE UNIVARIATE used:

       real time            0.99 seconds

16

17    ODS OUTPUT CLOSE;

18

19    %PUT The MEASURE_DSN macro variable contains the following data
sets &MEASURE_DSN..;

The MEASURE_DSN macro variable contains the following data sets MYLIB.MEASURE
MYLIB.MEASURE1.
```

Output 4.2 *Partial SAS log for Example 4.2*

❶ The MATCH_ALL= option in the ODS OUTPUT statement creates separate SAS data sets for each output object. The MATCH_ALL= option can also be used with BY-group processing. The macro variable MEASURE_DSN is created to store the names of each data set that is generated.

❷ Because two variables, WEIGHT and HEIGHT, are being analyzed, ODS produces output objects for each variable.

Without the MATCH_ALL= option, additional rows containing the results from HEIGHT would be included in the MYLIB.MEASURE data set.

With the MATCH_ALL= option, however, the MYLIB.MEASURE data set contains the results of the WEIGHT variable, and the MYLIB.MEASURE1 data set contains the results of the HEIGHT variable. In addition, the macro variable MEASURE_DSN contains the names of the two data sets.

The names of the new data sets are determined by using the MYLIB.MEASURE primary data set name as the common root name and then attaching a numeric suffix. The numeric suffix value is incremented by 1 for each new data set created. The order of the variables in the VAR statement determines which variable results are stored in which data set. If the primary data set name had ended in a number (like MYLIG.MEASUR10), then ODS would have used that number as the start (producing MYLIB.MEASUR10 and MYLIB.MEASUR11).

The MATCH_ALL= option can be applied to more than one object.

See Also

Section 3.2 "Identifying Output Objects with the ODS TRACE statement".

Chapter 5 "Working with ODS Destinations and Objects" when you are creating multiple output objects.

More Information

Chapters 7 and 8 of *Output Delivery System: The Basics* have more information about how to control the output data set names using the MATCH_ALL= option for each variable and for BY-group processing.

Working with ODS Destinations and Objects

5.1 Introduction to Working with Destinations and Objects

In some circumstances, for example, when BY statements are present, ODS might create multiple instances of an object. Multiple instances of objects can also be created by multiple analysis variables, or by multiple analyses within a PROC step. For objects that contain similar information, these multiple object instances have the same primary object name but different object pathnames. As in Example 5.2, the object pathnames

```
UNIVARIATE.BYGROUP1.WEIGHT.BASICMEASURES
UNIVARIATE.BYGROUP2.WEIGHT.BASICMEASURES
```

have the primary object name BASICMEASURES even though they are two separate objects. ODS does this to provide you with control over the information you can select.

Depending on your requirements, you have the flexibility to select all of the instances of the object by referencing the primary object's name or to select a specific instance by referencing the object's pathname. This is significant when multiple objects with the same object name are created.

When you use the OUTPUT destination, ODS provides options such as the MATCH_ALL= option for automatically saving multiple instances of an object as multiple data sets. This enables you to combine or subset data sets before generating the final output file.

5.2 Routing Objects to Multiple Destinations

The ability to route individual objects to selected destinations offers great flexibility for file generation and content. Any objects created by a SAS procedure can be selected. Any destination can be used and more than two destinations can be opened at a time. In the following example, the BasicMeasures object is selected for the HTML destination and the ExtremeObs object is selected for the RTF destination.

Example 5.1: Working with objects and several different destinations

```
ODS HTML FILE = 'C:\ODSRSLTS\BASIC_DEMOG.HTML' ;  ❶

ODS HTML SELECT BASICMEASURES;


ODS RTF FILE= 'C:\ODSRSLTS\EXTREME_DEMOG.RTF' ;  ❷

ODS RTF SELECT EXTREMEOBS;


PROC UNIVARIATE DATA=DEMOG;

    VAR WEIGHT;

RUN;  ❸


ODS RTF CLOSE;  ❹

ODS HTML CLOSE;
```

❶ The HTML destination is opened and the BasicMeasures object is selected.

❷ The RTF destination is opened and the ExtremeObs object is selected.

❸ ODS routes the information to the different destinations when the procedure executes (BasicMeasures results to the HTML destination and the ExtremeObs results to the RTF destination).

❹ The RTF and HTML destinations are closed.

The HTML file that is generated by Example 5.1 is shown in the following output:

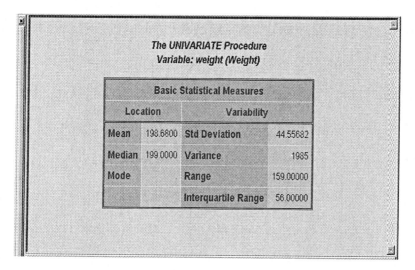

Output 5.1 *Contents of BASIC_DEMOG.HTML*

The RTF file that is generated by Example 5.1 is shown in the following output:

The SAS System

The UNIVARIATE Procedure
Variable: weight (Weight)

Extreme Observations			
Lowest		Highest	
Value	Obs	Value	Obs
111	22	236	19
116	6	255	20
117	13	257	1
150	7	264	3
162	25	270	4

Output 5.2 *Contents of EXTREME_DEMOG.RTF*

5.3 Managing Multiple Objects Generated with BY Statements

When you use the BY statement, ODS creates multiple instances of each object generated by the SAS procedure. Since multiple instances of an object share an object name, it is better to select an object by its pathname. In the DEMOG data set, there are two drugs used in the study. As a result of the BY statement, object instances will be created for each drug group. In this example, although the BasicMeasures object is now generated for each drug group, only the results from the first drug group are saved to the HTML file.

Example 5.2: Working with several objects from the BY Statement

```
PROC SORT DATA=DEMOG;

    BY DRUG;

RUN;



ODS HTML FILE='C:\ODSRSLTS\SELECT_WEIGHT_GROUP1_DEMOG.HTML';

ODS HTML SELECT UNIVARIATE.BYGROUP1.WEIGHT.BASICMEASURES;  ❶


PROC UNIVARIATE DATA=DEMOG;

    BY DRUG;  ❷

    VAR WEIGHT;

RUN;

ODS HTML CLOSE;
```

❶ To select the UNIVARIATE.BYGROUP1.WEIGHT.BASICMEASURES object to be included in the HTML file, the ODS HTML SELECT statement is used. In this example, the object pathname is referenced to include only the BasicMeasures results of the first drug group. If you had selected the BasicMeasures object, then the results of both drug groups would be written to the HTML file. If the OUTPUT destination had been used with the BasicMeasures object selected, then the data set created would have contained records from the results of both drug groups.

The tables below show the difference in the information selected by referencing the object's name and by referencing the object's full pathname when using the BY statement.

REFERENCE BY OBJECT NAME	OBJECT'S CONTENT
BASICMEASURES	Analysis results for GROUP 1 and GROUP 2

REFERENCE BY OBJECT'S FULL PATHNAME	OBJECT'S CONTENT
UNIVARIATE.BYGROUP1.WEIGHT.BASICMEASURES	Analysis results for GROUP 1
UNIVARIATE.BYGROUP2.WEIGHT.BASICMEASURES	Analysis results for GROUP 2

Remember to first use the ODS TRACE statement to list all output objects created if you do not know which objects to select or what the object's attributes are.

❷ The BY DRUG statement causes ODS to create multiple instances of an object. Since there are two drugs in the data set, there will be two sets of objects with the same object names. ODS adds the term BYGROUP to the object's pathname to differentiate the two sets of objects. The suffix to the term BYGROUP is increased by 1 for each unique DRUG value.

The HTML file that is generated by Example 5.2 is shown in the following output:

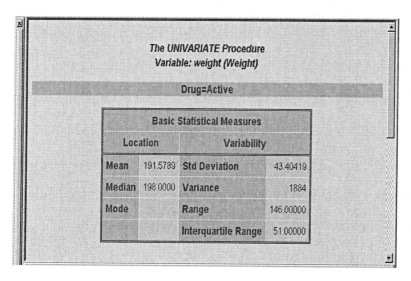

Output 5.3 *Contents of SELECT_WEIGHT_GROUP1_DEMOG.HTML*

5.4 Managing Object Instances Generated by Multiple Analysis Variables

In general, when you specify multiple analysis variables, ODS creates multiple instances of the objects with the execution of the SAS procedure. When multiple objects are created, it is generally easier to select an object by its pathname.

Example 5.3: Working with several objects from several analysis variables

```
ODS HTML FILE='C:\ODSRSLTS\SELECT_UNIVARIATE_DEMOG.HTML';


ODS HTML SELECT UNIVARIATE.WEIGHT.BASICMEASURES

                UNIVARIATE.HEIGHT.EXTREMEOBS;    ❶


PROC UNIVARIATE DATA=DEMOG;

     VAR WEIGHT HEIGHT;   ❷

RUN;

ODS HTML CLOSE;
```

❶ The ODS HTML SELECT statement selects the BasicMeasures results of the WEIGHT variable and the ExtremeObs results of the HEIGHT variable to be included in the HTML file. If you had selected the object's name, BasicMeasures, then the BasicMeasures results of both WEIGHT and HEIGHT would be included in the HTML file.

The tables below show the difference in the information that is selected by referencing the object's name and by referencing the object's full pathname when you use multiple analysis variables.

REFERENCE BY OBJECT'S NAME	OBJECT'S CONTENT
BASICMEASURES	Analysis results for WEIGHT and HEIGHT

REFERENCE BY OBJECT'S FULL PATHNAME	OBJECT'S CONTENT
UNIVARIATE.WEIGHT.BASICMEASURES	Analysis results for WEIGHT
UNIVARIATE.HEIGHT.BASICMEASURES	Analysis results for HEIGHT

Remember to first use the ODS TRACE statement to list all the output objects that are created if you do not know which objects to select or what the object's attributes are.

❷ The multiple analysis variables cause ODS to create multiple instances of an object. Since there are two analysis variables, there will be two sets of objects with the same object names. ODS adds the variable's name to the object's pathname to differentiate the two sets of objects.

The top portion of the HTML file containing the WEIGHT BasicMeasures results is shown in the following output:

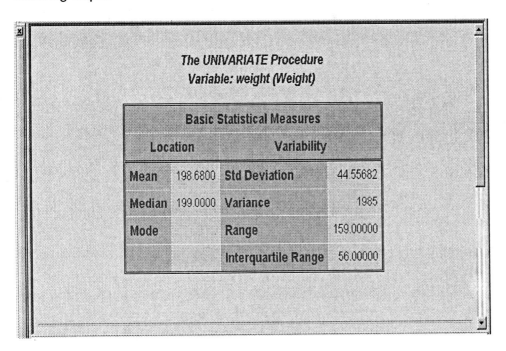

Basic Statistical Measures			
Location		**Variability**	
Mean	198.6800	**Std Deviation**	44.55682
Median	199.0000	**Variance**	1985
Mode	.	**Range**	159.00000
		Interquartile Range	56.00000

The UNIVARIATE Procedure
Variable: weight (Weight)

Output 5.4 *Top portion of SELECT_ UNIVARIATE _DEMOG.HTML*

The bottom portion of the same HTML file containing the HEIGHT ExtremeObs results is shown in the following output:

The SAS System

The UNIVARIATE Procedure
Variable: height (Height)

Extreme Observations			
Lowest		Highest	
Value	Obs	Value	Obs
56.7	6	72.4	25
57.7	16	73.0	15
58.9	22	73.6	12
59.8	13	74.4	1

Output 5.5 *Bottom portion of SELECT_ UNIVARIATE _DEMOG.HTML*

See Also

See the MATCH_ALL= option in Section 4.3 "Creating Multiple Data Sets" to learn how to save each table as a separate data set. However, if a single data set is needed, then this approach might require you to manually combine all the individual data sets into one data set.

CHAPTER 6

Enhancing Reports with ODS Styles

6.1 What Styles Can Do

Styles offer you choices for enhancing your output by enabling you to specify the report's presentation attributes, including fonts, colors, and alignment. ODS uses these attributes to specify the display of items such as titles, headers, and data. For example, different styles can use different fonts such as Times, Courier, Arial, or Helvetica, as well as different colors.

When you route ODS output to a destination that supports style attributes, ODS processes all output objects using presentation instructions (i.e., styles) for file creation. When a style is specified in the ODS statement, that style's predefined fonts, colors, and alignments will be used when the file is created.

The following table lists which destinations support styles. It makes sense that the LISTING and the OUTPUT destinations do not support styles because these destinations cannot take advantage of style attributes when they create the corresponding standard SAS listing output or a SAS data set. The other destinations, however, can apply style attributes.

DESTINATION	SUPPORT STYLE
HTML	Yes
RTF	Yes
LISTING	No
PRINTER, PS, PDF, and PCL	Yes
OUTPUT	No

Table 6.1 *Style support by destination*

6.2 Selection of a SAS-Supplied Style

For the destinations that support styles, ODS uses a different default style for each destination. ODS does this to take advantage of the unique differences between the destinations. For example, styles that are most appropriate for the HTML destination are more effective for viewing results on screens, while styles that are most appropriate for the PRINTER destination are more effective for printing high quality text-based output.

In addition to the default style for each destination, you have access to a collection of several SAS-supplied styles. These SAS-supplied styles are included during the installation process and do not require any additional setup. These styles can be used to produce great looking reports.

The following table lists a collection of SAS-supplied styles that can be used with the STYLE= option. Styles can be easily selected, enabling you to quickly see which style is best for your results. Although any style can be used with any destination that supports styles, in general, styles can be grouped together for the purpose of viewing, editing, or printing.

PURPOSE	NAME	DESCRIPTION
Screen Display for Viewing	BarrettsBlue	Blue header background, light table background
	Beige	Beige header text, white text in table
	Brick	Brick color header text, white text in table
	Brown	Brown title, black header, light table background
	D3D	White header, bold table border
	Default	Dark blue header, shade table background (Default for HTML Destination)
	NoFontDefault	Black header text, white background table
Text-Based Output for Editing	RTF	RTF style (Default for RTF Destination)
	Minimal	No color, light text in table
	Statdoc	Blue header, black text in table
	Theme	Dark header, dark table
Text-Based Output for Printing	Printer	Printer style (Default for PRINTER Destination)
	FancyPrinter	Printer style – *Italic font*, no bold labels, no color other than grey scale headers
	SansPrinter	Printer style – Times New Roman font, **bold labels**, no color other than grey scale, no grid table lines
	SasdocPrinter	Printer style – Times New Roman font, **bold labels**, no color, grid table lines
	SerifPrinter	Printer style – *Italic font* title, Times New Roman font, **bold labels**, no color other than grey scale, no grid table lines

Table 6.2 *SAS-supplied styles*

Example 6.1: Using ODS styles with destinations

```
ODS HTML FILE='C:\ODSRSLTS\DEMOG_STYLE.HTML' STYLE=SASDOCPRINTER;  ❶


PROC UNIVARIATE DATA=DEMOG;

    VAR WEIGHT;

RUN;

ODS HTML CLOSE;
```

❶ The STYLE= option selects the SasDocPrinter SAS-supplied style to define the HTML destination's style attributes. By changing the STYLE= specification in the ODS statement, the HTML file is enhanced with the style's predefined color combination, fonts, and alignment. As you can see in the following output, the output can be more visually appealing while the content remains unchanged. Note that any destination supporting styles could be used with any SAS-supplied or user-created style. However, some styles work better with some destinations than with others.

A portion of the HTML file that is generated by Example 6.1 is shown in the following output:

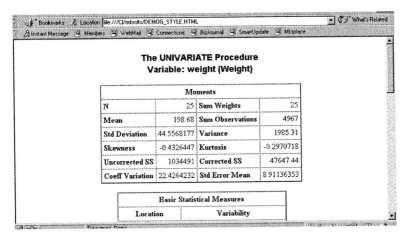

Output 6.1 *Portion of DEMOG_STYLE.HTML*

References

SAS Documentation

SAS Institute Inc. 1999. *The Complete Guide to the SAS Output Delivery System, Version 8.* Cary, NC: SAS Institute Inc.

Haworth, Lauren E. *Output Delivery System: The Basics.* Cary, NC: SAS Institute Inc. 2001.

Articles and Papers

Gupta, Sunil. 2000. "Customized Reports with SAS ODS." *Proceedings of the Eighth Annual Western Users of SAS Software*, Scottsdale, AZ.

Gupta, Sunil. 2002. "Quick Results with the Output Delivery System." *Proceedings of the Twenty-Seventh Annual SAS Users Group International Conference*, Orlando, FL.

Gupta, Sunil. 2002. "Using Styles and Templates to Customize SAS ODS Output." *Proceedings of the Twenty-Seventh Annual SAS Users Group International Conference*, Orlando, FL.

Lafler, Kirk Paul, 2000. "Creating HTML Output with the Output Delivery System." *Proceedings of the Twenty-Fifth Annual SAS Users Group International Conference*, Indianapolis, IN.

McNeill, Sandy. 2000. "ODS for Dummies." *Proceedings of the Eighth Annual Western Users of SAS Software Conference*, Scottsdale, AZ.

Olinger, Chris. 2000 "ODS for Dummies." *Proceedings of the Twenty-Fifth Annual SAS Users Group International Conference*, Indianapolis, IN.

Appendix

DEMOG Data Set

The DEMOG data set is the data set that is used in all of the examples in this book. It contains information about patients in a clinical trial study. Each patient has the following data: gender, height, weight, age, race, and drug taken.

```
libname mylib 'c:\odsrslts';
```

```
data mylib.demog;

   input patient $3. gender 3. height 4.1 weight 4. age 5.1

       race 3. drug $7.;

   format height age 4.1;

   label patient='Patient' gender='Sex' height='Height'

       weight='Weight' age='Age' race='Race' drug='Drug';

datalines;

001 1 74.4 257 67.9 1 Active
002 1 63.1 168 36.7 0 Active
003 1 69.6 264 74.6 0 Placebo
004 1 63.2 270 73.8 1 Placebo
005 1 67.8 209 57.8 1 Active
006 0 56.7 116 47.5 1 Active
007 1 70.4 150 47.8 1 Active
008 1 68.5 172 82.6 1 Active
009 0 66.4 212 25.1 0 Active
010 1 68.1 216 60.6 1 Placebo
011 1 62.8 193 80.0 1 Active
012 1 73.6 198 77.4 1 Active
013 0 59.8 117 72.3 1 Active
014 0 74.7 179 37.4 0 Placebo
```

```
015 1 73.0 195 21.4 1 Active
016 1 57.7 213 27.3 1 Active
017 1 59.9 199 43.1 1 Active
018 1 70.2 219 67.3 0 Active
019 1 68.6 236 62.2 1 Placebo
020 1 70.7 255 66.4 1 Active
021 1 71.6 228 27.3 1 Active
022 1 58.9 111 68.3 1 Active
023 1 65.7 194 67.1 0 Active
024 1 63.2 234 65.2 0 Active
025 1 72.4 162 56.1 0 Placebo
;
run;
```

Index

Books Available from SAS Press

Advanced Log-Linear Models Using SAS®
by **Daniel Zelterman** . . . . Order No. A57496

Analysis of Clinical Trials Using SAS®: A Practical
Guide
by **Alex Dmitrienko, Walter Offen,**
Christy Chuang-Stein,
and **Geert Molenbergs** . . . . Order No. A59390

Annotate: Simply the Basics
by **Art Carpenter** . . . . Order No. A57320

Applied Multivariate Statistics with SAS® Software,
Second Edition
by **Ravindra Khattree**
and **Dayanand N. Naik** . . . . Order No. A56903

Applied Statistics and the SAS® Programming
Language, Fourth Edition
by **Ronald P. Cody**
and **Jeffrey K. Smith** . . . . Order No. A55984

An Array of Challenges — Test Your SAS® Skills
by **Robert Virgile** . . . . Order No. A55625

Carpenter's Complete Guide to the SAS® Macro
Language, Second Edition
by **Art Carpenter** . . . . Order No. A59224

The Cartoon Guide to Statistics
by **Larry Gonick**
and **Woollcott Smith** . . . . Order No. A5515

Categorical Data Analysis Using the SAS® System,
Second Edition
by **Maura E. Stokes, Charles S. Davis,**
and **Gary G. Koch** . . . . Order No. A57998

Cody's Data Cleaning Techniques Using SAS® Software
by **Ron Cody** . . . . Order No. A57198

Common Statistical Methods for Clinical Research
with SAS® Examples, Second Edition
by **Glenn A. Walker** . . . . Order No. A58086

Debugging SAS® Programs: A Handbook of Tools
and Techniques
by **Michele M. Burlew** . . . . Order No. A57743

Efficiency: Improving the Performance of Your SAS®
Applications
by **Robert Virgile** . . . . Order No. A55960

The Essential PROC SQL Handbook for SAS® Users
by **Katherine Prairie** . . . . Order No. A58546

Fixed Effects Regression Methods for Longitudinal
Data Using SAS®
by **Paul D. Allison** . . . . Order No. A58348

Genetic Analysis of Complex Traits Using SAS®
Edited by **Arnold M. Saxton** . . . . Order No. A59454

A Handbook of Statistical Analyses Using SAS®,
Second Edition
by **B.S. Everitt**
and **G. Der** . . . . Order No. A58679

Health Care Data and the SAS® System
by **Marge Scerbo, Craig Dickstein,**
and **Alan Wilson** . . . . Order No. A57638

The How-To Book for SAS/GRAPH® Software
by **Thomas Miron** . . . . Order No. A55203

Instant ODS: Style Templates for the Output
Delivery System
by **Bernadette Johnson** . . . . Order No. A58824

In the Know... SAS® Tips and Techniques From Around
the Globe
by **Phil Mason** . . . . Order No. A55513

support.sas.com/pubs

support.sas.com/pubs

*SAS® System for Elementary Statistical Analysis,
Second Edition*
by **Sandra D. Schlotzhauer**
and **Ramon C. Littell**. . . . . Order No. A55172

SAS® System for Mixed Models
by **Ramon C. Littell, George A. Milliken, Walter W.
Stroup,** and **Russell D. Wolfinger** . . Order No. A55235

SAS® System for Regression, Second Edition
by **Rudolf J. Freund**
and **Ramon C. Littell**. . . . . Order No. A56141

SAS® System for Statistical Graphics, First Edition
by **Michael Friendly** . . . . Order No. A56143

The SAS® Workbook and Solutions Set
(books in this set also sold separately)
by **Ron Cody** . . . . Order No. A55594

*Selecting Statistical Techniques for Social Science
Data: A Guide for SAS® Users*
by **Frank M. Andrews, Laura Klem, Patrick M. O'Malley,
Willard L. Rodgers, Kathleen B. Welch,**
and **Terrence N. Davidson** . . . . Order No. A55854

Statistical Quality Control Using the SAS® System
by **Dennis W. King**. . . . . Order No. A55232

*A Step-by-Step Approach to Using the SAS® System
for Factor Analysis and Structural Equation Modeling*
by **Larry Hatcher**. . . . . Order No. A55129

*A Step-by-Step Approach to Using the SAS® System
for Univariate and Multivariate Statistics,
Second Edition*
by **Larry Hatcher, Norm O'Rourke,**
and **Edward J. Stepanski** . . . . Order No. A58929

*Step-by-Step Basic Statistics Using SAS®: Student
Guide and Exercises*
(books in this set also sold separately)
by **Larry Hatcher**. . . . . Order No. A57541

*Survival Analysis Using the SAS® System:
A Practical Guide*
by **Paul D. Allison** . . . . Order No. A55233

*Tuning SAS® Applications in the OS/390 and z/OS
Environments, Second Edition*
by **Michael A. Raithel** . . . . Order No. A58172

*Univariate and Multivariate General Linear Models:
Theory and Applications Using SAS® Software*
by **Neil H. Timm**
and **Tammy A. Mieczkowski**. . . . . . . Order No. A55809

Using SAS® in Financial Research
by **Ekkehart Boehmer, John Paul Broussard,**
and **Juha-Pekka Kallunki** . . . . Order No. A57601

*Using the SAS® Windowing Environment:
A Quick Tutorial*
by **Larry Hatcher**. . . . . Order No. A57201

Visualizing Categorical Data
by **Michael Friendly** . . . . Order No. A56571

Web Development with SAS® by Example
by **Frederick Pratter** . . . . Order No. A58694

*Your Guide to Survey Research Using the
SAS® System*
by **Archer Gravely**. . . . . Order No. A55688

JMP® Books

*JMP® for Basic Univariate and Multivariate Statistics:
A Step-by-Step Guide*
by **Ann Lehman, Norm O'Rourke, Larry Hatcher,**
and **Edward J. Stepanski** . . . . Order No. A59814

JMP® Start Statistics, Third Edition
by **John Sall, Ann Lehman,**
and **Lee Creighton** . . . . Order No. A58166

Regression Using JMP®
by **Rudolf J. Freund, Ramon C. Littell,**
and **Lee Creighton** . . . . Order No. A58789

support.sas.com/pubs

Online Samples — Examples from This Book at Your Fingertips

Companion Web Sites

You can access the example programs for this book by linking to its Companion Web site: **support.sas.com/companionsites**. Select the book title to display its Companion Web site, then select **Example Code** to display the SAS programs that are included in the book.

Anonymous FTP

You can use anonymous FTP to download ASCII files and binary files (SAS data libraries in transport format). To use anonymous FTP, connect to FTP.SAS.COM and enter the following responses as you are prompted:

Name (ftp.sas.com:user-id): anonymous
Password: <your e-mail address>

When you are logged on, download one or more example program files to your local directory:

get /pub/publications/A##### <your-local-filename>
(for ASCII files) or

get /pub/publications/B##### <your-local-filename>
(for binary files)

where ##### is the 5-digit order number that appears on the front cover of the book. If you need a list of all available example files, download the file **/pub/publications/index**.

SASDOC-L Listserv

Through the SASDOC-L listserv, you can download ASCII files of example programs from this book. By subscribing to SASDOC-L, you also receive notification when example programs from a new book become available.

To subscribe to SASDOC-L, send e-mail with a blank subject line to **LISTSERV@VM.SAS.COM.** The body of the message should be

SUBSCRIBE SASDOC-L *<firstname lastname>*

To download the file for a book, send this message to **SASDOC-L@VM.SAS.COM:**

get A##### examples sasdoc-l

where ##### is the 5-digit order number that appears on the front cover of the book.

Comments or Questions?

If you have comments or questions about this book, you may contact the author through SAS by

Mail: SAS Institute Inc.
SAS Press
Attn: <Author's name>
SAS Campus Drive
Cary, NC 27513

E-mail: saspress@sas.com

Fax: (919) 677-8166

Please include the title of the book in your correspondence.

See the last pages of this book for a complete list of books available through **SAS Press** or visit **support.sas.com/pubs.**

Titles in Art Carpenter's SAS® Software Series

***Quick Results with the
Output Delivery System***
by Sunil K. Gupta
(Order No. A58458)

Annotate: Simply the Basics
by Art Carpenter
(Order No. A57320)

***Multiple-Plot Displays:
Simplified with Macros***
by Perry Watts
(Order No. A58314)

***Maps Made Easy
Using SAS®***
by Mike Zdeb
(Order No. A57495)

To order: support.sas.com/pubs
Or call: (800) 727-3228

Printed in the United States
27828LVS00002B/53